A New True Book

CUBA

By Karen Jacobsen

Flag of Cuba

CHILDRENS PRESS®

CHICAGO

Young Cubans in Havana

PHOTO CREDITS

AP/Wide World Photos—23, 27 (2 photos), 41 (left), 44

© Cameramann International, Ltd.—34 (left)

Reprinted with permission of *The New Book of Knowledge*, 1989 edition, © Grolier Inc.—5

Historical Pictures Service, Chicago—18 (2 photos), 19 (left), 21

© Hutchison Library—17, 30; © Christine Pemberton, 33 (left)

Chip and Rosa Maria de la Cueva Peterson—© Phillips Bourns, 2, 10, 12 (bottom right), 31 (right), 39 (left), 41 (right), 45 (left)

Root Resources—© Paul Conklin, 7, 11 (left), 13 (right), 25 (left), 29 (right and bottom left), 34 (right), 36 (2 photos), 38, 39 (right), 45 (right)

Shostal Associates/SuperStock International, Inc.—9, 12 (top left and top right), 24 (2 photos), 25 (right), 33 (top right)

© Sovfoto—19 (right), 28 (left), 42 (left)

Tom Stack & Associates—© Malcolm Gilson, Cover, 13 (left), 14 (2 photos), 29 (top left), 35

© Lauren Stockbower—28 (right), 42 (right), 40

Valan—© Y. R. Tymstra, 11 (right), 12 (bottom left), 37; © Don McPhee, 31 (bottom left); © Kennon Cooke, 31 (top left); © Anthony Scullion, 33 (bottom right)

Cover — Valle de Vinales, Pinar del Rio, Cuba

Library of Congress Cataloging-in-Publication Data

Jacobsen, Karen.
  Cuba / by Karen Jacobsen.
    p.   cm. — (A New true book)
  Includes index.
  Summary: Examines the history, modern life, industries, arts, sports, and geography of Cuba.
  ISBN-0-516-01183-9
  1. Cuba—Juvenile literature. [1. Cuba.]
I. Title.
F1758.5.J33 1990   89-25426
972.91—dc20   CIP
                                     AC

TABLE OF CONTENTS

CUBA IN THE WORLD

Cuba is south of North America and north of South America. Cuba is an island country. It has one main island, one smaller island, and more than 1,600 very small islands.

Cuba's main island is almost 750 miles long. It is shaped like a long fish or an alligator.

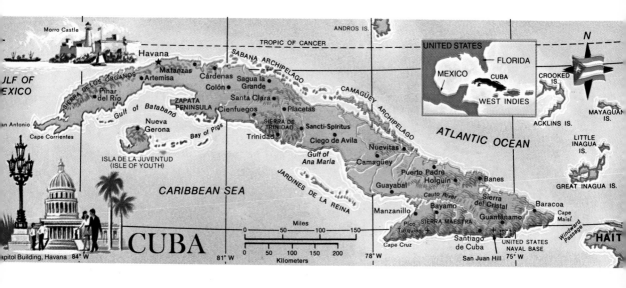

Cuba's second largest island is Isla de la Juventud, or the Isle of Youth. It is about 50 miles wide.

Three large bodies of water surround Cuba: they are the Atlantic Ocean, the Caribbean Sea, and the Gulf of Mexico. Cuba is in the middle of some of the world's most important shipping routes.

Cuba's nearest neighbors are Mexico (about 130 miles to the west), the United States of America (about 90 miles to the north), the Bahamas (about 100 miles to the north), Haiti (about 50 miles to the east), and Jamaica (about 90 miles to the south).

A LAND OF
NATURAL BEAUTY

In many places along
Cuba's coastline, there are
fine beaches, coral reefs,
and mangrove swamps.

Cuba receives plenty of
rain and sunshine. It is

never cold. Cuba has more
than three thousand kinds of
trees, flowers, and other plants.

Flat plains, rolling hills,
and several mountain ranges
cover most of Cuba.

The Organos Mountains
are in the west. They have
unusual shapes. Some look
like organ pipes, others look
like haystacks. There are
many small caves and a few
large caverns in the mountains.

The Sierra de Trinidad and
Escambray mountains in the

The Escambray range crosses central Cuba.

center of Cuba are known
for their deep valleys, and
their waterfalls and lakes.

On the eastern end of the
island, the Sierra Maestra rise
up from the sea. Pico Turquino,
on the south coast, is 6,560
feet high. It is the highest
point in Cuba.

IMPORTANT CITIES

Havana is built on a bay in northwest Cuba. It has an excellent harbor and is Cuba's largest city. More than two million people live there.

A lighthouse stands at the entrance to Havana's harbor.

Examples of Spanish colonial architecture are found throughout Havana.

Some parts of Havana are very old. They were built in Spanish colonial times. But most of Havana is modern, with wide avenues and high-rise buildings.

More than two million people
live and work in Havana,
the capital city of Cuba.

Cathedral (left) and
city street (right)
in Santiago, Cuba.

Santiago de Cuba in
eastern Cuba was founded
in 1540, one year before
Havana. With more than
three hundred thousand
people, it is the second
largest city in Cuba.

High rise for workers (left) and view of
Santiago looking toward the harbor (right)

Santiago is built on
hillsides. Its streets wind
upward from the busy harbor
below. Much of old Santiago
still looks as it did long ago.
But new factories, schools,
and apartments have been
14   built outside the city.

CUBA LONG AGO

The first people lived in Cuba about 3500 B.C. Their cave drawings have been found.

Much later, other tribes came in canoes from South America. In Cuba, the tribes fished and hunted. They also harvested fruits and vegetables. They built their houses from the trunks and leaves of palm trees.

COLUMBUS STARTS A SPANISH COLONY

In 1492, Christopher Columbus and his men were the first Europeans to see Cuba. They thought they were in India or Japan. Instead, they had discovered a new world.

Columbus claimed Cuba for Spain. He said that Cuba was "the most beautiful land" that he had ever seen.

At first, the people who

Sugarcane and tobacco grow quickly in Cuba's fertile soil.

came from Spain looked for gold, silver, and jewels. But they discovered that Cuba's wealth was in its rich, red soil. They decided to grow sugarcane and tobacco to sell in Europe.

The Spanish forced the native people to plant crops.

17

Hernando Cortés (right) and Diego Velázquez conquered Cuba for Spain in 1511. The Spanish killed Chief Hatuey (left) because he led the Indians against the Spaniards.

But, in a short time, the natives were all dead. They were killed by cruel treatment and by the strange diseases brought to Cuba by the Spaniards.

The landowners then brought slaves from Africa. The slaves lived a very hard life on the plantations.

Thousands of African slaves died because they were beaten by their owners (above) or overworked in the sugarcane fields (left).

Sugar and tobacco grew well in Cuba's hot, moist climate. For more than 200 years, Spanish ships carried Cuban crops and South American treasure to Spain. The ships returned with supplies and soldiers from Spain or with more slaves from Africa.

THE FIGHT FOR INDEPENDENCE

In the 1800s, the Spanish colonies of Mexico, Peru, and Argentina won their independence from Spain.

Some Cubans wanted independence for Cuba, too. Again and again they fought against Spanish troops. But they always lost.

In 1898, a United States battleship, the *Maine*, blew up in Havana's harbor. Most of its crew members were killed.

When the *Maine* sank in Havana's harbor, the *New York Journal* offered a $50,000 reward for the capture of the people responsible for the explosion.

The United States blamed Spain for the explosion. They declared war and defeated the Spanish army. Spain no longer owned Cuba. Cuba belonged to the United States. And the Cubans still did not have freedom.

In 1902, the United States allowed Cuba to form its own government. But the United States stayed, ready to take over again if there was any trouble.

During the next 30 years, the government of Cuba changed many times— sometimes with elections and other times with bullets. The United States took over twice, in 1906 and in 1921. Both times the United States returned Cuba to its elected leaders.

BATISTA RULES CUBA

In 1933, Sergeant Fulgencio Batista and some soldiers in the Cuban army took over.

In 1940, Batista was elected president. At the end of his term, he left Cuba. But he returned in 1952. Under

In 1940, Colonel Fulgencio Batista was elected president of Cuba.

Hotel Habana Libre (left) and a beach at a resort hotel in Varadero (right)

Batista, wealthy Cubans and Americans owned Cuba's hotels, banks, and plantations. Havana became a gambling center. Tourists from all over the world came to Cuba for its sun and fun.

The wealthy people made money. But the Cuban people were poor. They did not own anything. They needed jobs, medical care, and housing. They could not read or write.

Many of the Cuban people live in small villages and towns such as Trinidad (right).

THE REVOLUTION

In 1953, Fidel Castro and his supporters attacked a military barracks at Santiago de Cuba. But they were captured and put in jail.

When Castro got out of jail, he went to Mexico.

In 1956, Castro and his supporters sailed back to Cuba. They camped in the

Fidel Castro (right) and his supporters lived in hiding
and attacked the Batista government from 1956 to 1959.
Castro's revolution was supported by the poor
people who hoped for a better future.

Sierra Maestra and started a
revolution against Batista.

In 1959, Batista gave up.
Fidel Castro took over the
government. Castro put the
people who disagreed with
him in jail.

When Castro (above) declared Cuba a Communist country, he turned to Russia for help. On May Day (right), an important international Communist holiday, the Cuban people honor Russian as well as Cuban revolutionaries.

COMMUNIST CUBA

In 1960, Fidel Castro declared Cuba to be a Communist country. Castro said that the wealth of Cuba would be shared by all its people.

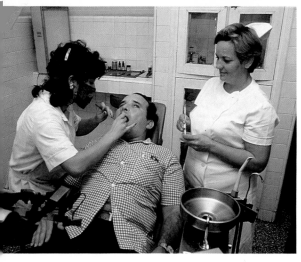

The Russians sent materials for this workers' apartment building (top left). Castro's government has worked to improve health care (left) and education (above).

Today there is free education, free health care, and low-cost housing in Cuba. More than 90 percent of the people can read and write.

CUBA TODAY

There are more than ten million people in Cuba. Most Cubans are descendants of Spanish settlers. Many are descendants of Africans or of mixed Spanish and African ancestors. In Cuba today, all races are equal. The national language is Spanish.

Teacher directs a school band that features guitars and bongo drums.

Cuba's cattle are a combination of Brahman cattle (above left) and Holstein cows (left). Its fishing fleet travels the seven seas.

Cuba has a modern fishing fleet. Its workers fish in all of the world's oceans.

Cuba's cattle herds are increasing. Its milk cows are a combination of Holsteins (to give plenty of milk) and Brahmans from India (to

31

resist the heat). Cuba's cattle herds provide beef and leather.

Cuba is trying to develop more small industries, to create jobs and make products for Cubans.

Cuba has a large supply of nickel. The export of nickel is an important industry in Cuba.

Coffee, tobacco, and citrus fruits are sold to other countries around the world.

Sugarcane (above left and right) and
tobacco (right) are raised on large plantations.

Cuba's most important
crop is sugarcane. After
many processing steps, the
cane sugar becomes white
sugar crystals.

The leftover cane fiber is
used as fuel in the mills. It

is also made into paper. One out of every four Cubans works in the sugarcane industry.

Cuba sells much of its food to other countries. It uses the money it gets from food to buy the things it needs.

Because the government

Because Cuba sells its food to other countries to raise money, food is expensive and long food lines are common.

All schoolchildren receive free lunches.

needs money, it controls
most of Cuba's food supply.
Everybody in Cuba is
supposed to be able to buy
the same amount, and no
more. But many people are
unhappy because they want
more.

There is not enough good housing for all Cubans. In many towns, the government supplies the building materials. Then carpenters, bricklayers, plumbers, and electricians work with volunteers to build new houses.

Working with experts, volunteers build houses.

The walls and roof of this house were made from the wood and leaves of palm trees.

In the country, many people live in "bohios." Bohios are like the thatch-roofed houses that the native Cubans lived in long ago. Bohios usually have two rooms. A separate hut serves as the cooking area.

EDUCATION

Education is free for every child in Cuba. There are day-care centers to take care of very young children.

From the seventh to the tenth grade, most students attend secondary schools. Secondary students spend half of the schoolday in class and the other half at work.

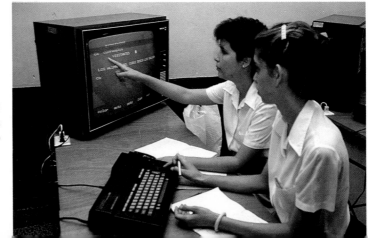

A high school computer class in Santiago

About the Author

Karen Jacobsen is a graduate of the University of Connecticut and Syracuse University. She has been a teacher and is a writer. She likes to find out about interesting subjects and then write about them.

revolution(reh • voh • LOO • shun) —a sudden change in the
     government of a country
route(ROOT) —a path or course to follow on a journey
slavery(SLAYV • er • ee) —the practice of owning people
South America(SOWTH ah • MER • ih • ka) —a continent with
     the South Atlantic Ocean on the east and South
     Pacific on the west; also, with North America to the
     north
swamp(SWAHMP) —a wet, marshy land
treasure(TREJ • er) —a collection of valuable things

INDEX

WORDS YOU SHOULD KNOW

barracks(BAR • aks) —buildings used as dormitories for soldiers or other groups of people

bay(BAY) —arm of the sea in a recessed curve of the shore

cavern(KAV • ern) —large, underground cave

Communist(KOM • yoo • nist) —way of government, requires equal common ownership of all property

coral(KOR • ul) —a hard substance, like stone, made of animal skeletons in tropical seas

crop(KROP) —plants grown for harvest as food

cruel(KROO • ul) —causing pain and suffering

descendants(dee • SEN • dants) —the offspring of an ancestor

gulf(GULF) —an arm of the sea

harbor(HAR • bur) —a sheltered part of a larger body of water

independence(in • dih • PEN • dense) —freedom from the control of another country or person

island(EYE • land) —a body of land surrounded by water

isle(EYL) —a small island

mangrove(MAN • grove) —a tropical shore tree

modern(MOD • ern) —up-to-date; recent

native(NAY • tiv) —born in or belonging to a place

North America(NORTH ah • MER • ih • ka) —the continent with the North Atlantic Ocean on the east and the North Pacific Ocean on the west; also, to the north of South America

plain(PLAYN) —a flat land area

range(RAYNJ) —a group of mountains

Changes happen very slowly in Cuba. The Cuban people are working hard to make their future better than their past. Cuba is still the "beautiful land" that Columbus wrote about so long ago.

For the poor, the revolution was a chance to change and improve their lives. But other Cubans hated the revolution and Fidel Castro. For them, it was the end of hope. They lost their homes, businesses, and freedom. Thousands of Cubans left Cuba to live in other countries.

Thousands of Cubans left Cuba when Castro took over. Tent cities were set up in Florida to give these people temporary shelter.

Before the 1959 revolution, most Cubans were Roman Catholics. But, in a Communist country, religious holidays are not celebrated.

In Cuba, most holidays remember the revolution. January 1 is New Year's Day and also the Anniversary of the Revolution. July 26 is the most important Cuban holiday. It celebrates the day Castro attacked the barracks in 1953. Many days of carnival dancing and parties lead up to July 26.

Drums are used to beat out
lively dance rhythms.

Cuban music combines
Spanish and African rhythms.
The conga and the rumba
are both Cuban dances.

Professional baseball players such as José Canseco (left)
first played on grade school teams (right) in Cuba.

THE PEOPLE OF CUBA

Cubans love baseball.
Every town has a team.
Cubans also enjoy boxing,
soccer (futbol), and jai alai.
Swimming, fishing, and
boating also are popular.

41

The government supports special schools for dance, art, and music. Many of their graduates become teachers.

talented students receive special training at Cuba's Sports Institute, the National School of Art, or the National School of Ballet.

Many Cuban adults work full-time and attend night classes to learn new skills.

Classes at Havana University Law School (above) and the campus of Lenin Vocational School (left)

Special secondary schools teach courses in subjects such as languages, technology, agriculture, or teacher-training. Graduates of these schools may go on to national universities.

A small number of